"As a city dweller, my initial interest in pressed flower arranging faded when I was confronted by the difficulties of obtaining many of the flowers used in standard arrangements . . . This feeling only vanished as I grew aware of the extraordinary range of plant life which flourishes in urban areas." – THE AUTHOR

THE MINIATURE WORLD OF
PRESSED
FLOWERS

Nona Pettersen

THE MINIATURE
WORLD OF
PRESSED
FLOWERS

Nona Pettersen

W I BOOKS LTD

SEARCH PRESS

First published 1986
Reprinted 1987
by Search Press Ltd
Wellwood
North Farm Road
Tunbridge Wells
Kent
TN2 3DR

ISBN 0 85532 578 X (pb)

Typeset by Phoenix Photosetting, Chatham, Kent
Printed in Italy by G. Canale & C. S.p.A. - Turin

Contents

Introduction

THE MINIATURE VIEW
OF THE URBAN GARDEN

All the flower arrangements in this book are based on a small or miniature scale. While skilled and attractive work can certainly be accomplished on a larger scale, the miniature is particularly suitable for the aspiring arranger, or anyone who does not have easy access to a garden or a regular supply of freshly picked flowers.

As a city dweller, my initial interest in pressed flower arranging faded when I was confronted by the difficulties of obtaining many of the flowers used in standard arrangements, or in the selection of cultivated varieties recommended by authors. As a result I dismissed the pressed flower medium from my mind as the perogative of the country dweller or of those fortunate enough to possess a town garden. This feeling only vanished as I grew aware of the extraordinary range of plant life which flourishes in urban areas – the curious cosmopolitan garden which flowers on derelict sites awaiting development, or around the borders of temporary car parks, along railway and canal banks, by neglected walls, fences and railings, between paving slabs and in cracks in concrete and in the grassed areas of community lawns, parks, playing grounds, sports fields and road verges.

Conventional arrangements are often restricted to a familiar range of flowers. The miniature, however, draws attention to the tiny plants which often lie unnoticed, precisely because of their diminutive size, while the search for suitable material can produce for all of us a fresh awareness of our everyday surroundings. Placed within a small area, for example, the little Scarlet Pimpernel suddenly acquires a new dimension and, from a miniaturist's viewpoint, a tangle of weeds is transformed into a field of colourful flowers. Tiny plant particles, easily overlooked when included in a large arrangement, provide significant details in the miniature and for the collector. A seeded Shepherd's Purse with glistening pods, for instance, can produce as much pleasure as the sighting of a rare breed of Orchid. Unlike the naturalist who requires a complete specimen for botanical reference, the arranger is free to select only that which appeals in shape or colour; and with a little experience you will become acquainted with the bewildering range of plants which all of which have something to contribute to a collection even when some seem determined to deceive you by their awkward shape and proportions.

Plants which look large or ungainly at first glance will frequently yield an intriguing crop of bracts, calyxes, stigmas, sepals, stamens and pods when examined more closely and gently taken apart – although it may be necessary to wait for the flowers and leaves to wither away before these shapes stand out clearly and acquire their subtle colouring.

When ripe the Common Sorrel, which grows on waste land, bears a brilliant galaxy of rust-red stars and once these magnificent fruits have been harvested, a previously derelict stretch becomes an exciting hunting ground as the search continues for similar surprises. The Red Valerian, which blazes on railway embankments, supports fire pink flowers on tough, thick branches which are impossible to press in complete form; only by breaking the branches into small segments can you obtain the slender purple flutes which emerge when dry from the press. The Red Clover, which grows in grass verges, is another plant whose dense clump flower heads seem designed to mislead the collector intent on small specimens — by splitting open the head with a thumbnail, you will find many tiny flowers curving from a stalk in the centre. This is only one example of an unlikely pressing flower which consists of tiny florets or corollas grouped tightly together, each one forming an ideal piece of miniature material when used individually.

On a regular routine walk through a built-up district it is easy for us to overlook the plant life which dwells in brick and stone crevices. Yet near to gutter pipes and gargoyles there are often clusters of ferns and moss mounds and often, slightly above eye-level, there are trails of Ivy and clumps of Ivy-leaved Toadflax with coiling stems and pale violet flowers. At ground level Red Deadnettles sprout between paving cracks; and if you pick one of these street weeds and examine it, you will find soft pink trumpet flowers concealed between downy, heart-shaped leaves.

Weaving through railings and fences are many straggling strands of Cleavers or Goosegrass which divide into distinctive dark stars and the variety of grasses which form elegant sprays when bleached by the sun. By looking with a fresh, enquiring eye at plants or weeds which are usually dismissed as commonplace, the miniaturist will discover a wealth of unusual material to be collected and, in return for a small amount of time taken in exploring an alternative route or walking

through an unfamiliar area, there is the prospect of being repaid with the occasional rarity.

While modern development is responsible for levelling large areas of urban land which were once occupied by tenants who took pride in their small back gardens and courtyard flower beds, traces of these buried gardens often survive and can be seen forcing their way through the surface of car parks regardless of the heavy trampling and traffic. In compensation, the motorist often contributes to collections by carrying seeds – caught in clothes, hair, and soles of shoes and the striations of tyres – over considerable distances. Eventually shaken free, these seeds can take root in districts far removed from their original habitat. In dockside and railway areas in fact, it is possible to find plants which have travelled from foreign lands.

From my personal point of view, it is this fascinating search for natural material that thrives amidst indifference and neglect, and the continual promise of unexpected discoveries, which turns the miniature into the most rewarding form of floral art.

Although there is sufficient variety within cities and towns to keep a keen collector in ample supplies throughout the year, you may wish also to use some of the smaller garden flowers which blossom during the spring and summer months. During my first collecting season, I was often frustrated by the sight of masses of bright flowers firmly embedded in private gardens and public parks. I managed to control my urge to pick them, however, except for those which had straggled or seeded themselves outside their original boundaries, which I regarded as fair game. I used to pick these in small quantities whenever the opportunity arose, until one day in a neighbouring village when I was confronted by an indignant lady who had watched me picking a few Periwinkles from a grass bank in front of her house. I was informed in no uncertain manner that all the flowers on the grass bank were her personal property, not public property to be plundered by city visitors to the countryside, and I made a swift retreat. Even so, I might have returned to my village bank raids had it not been for a visit the following year to a garden nursery on the outskirts of the city.

Boxes of bedding plants were on display and I came home with a selection of Lobelias and Alyssums which soon came into full flower when I placed them on a sunny ledge above my back yard.

These were clipped for pressing directly from the boxes and, within a few days, every available book had been consulted for information on window boxes, hanging baskets, and garden tubs, balcony, patio and roof gardening, terraniums, indoor plants and miniature gardens. Trays of Candytuft were raised from seed under glass, plants purchased from market stalls and nurseries were transferred into large polythene containers of tomato compost, plastic containers were converted into temporary tubs. My friends, surprised by this sudden interest in makeshift horticulture, soon arrived with selections of cuttings and sound advice on watering, temperature and suitable conditions. Species which could not be raised in windows or yard fashion came from a nearby florist, adding Sweet Williams, Montbretia, Delphinium, Larkspur and Tulips to the collection although it was necessary to explain why I wanted the flowers in dry condition and not refreshed by the mist sprays which are often used to revive wilting stock.

After a while I was allowed to forage through the florist's buckets of not so fresh flowers at the back of the shop for the petals from Roses, Carnations and some of the more exotic varieties which were still in good condition. Although many of these petals are much too large to be included in a miniature arrangement, they can be trimmed into small shapes such as vases, bows, ribbons and accessories or embossed to provide interesting textures for fabrics.

Because of the small scale, the collector will find a wide selection of material more useful than large quantities, and this can be gathered during the year whenever circumstances are suitable. For the arranger with limited leisure, the miniature will prove to be a particularly convenient form of presentation because only a few pieces are required to assemble a simple arrangement and this can be completed within a comparatively short space of time.

This book is designed to introduce the beginner to plant pressing and its potential uses, but I hope it will also persuade any disheartened student to return to an absorbing occupation with a renewed enthusiasm. For the expert, who already has a sound knowledge of pressed material, miniature work might well prove to be a refreshing change from the usual presentations, while some of the small-scale suggestions can be adapted to suit other scales and make use of material which is already in store.

CHAPTER ONE
Pressing materials

CHAPTER ONE

Pressing materials

Plants are preserved by the extraction of their natural moisture. With pressed plants, this can be done by placing freshly picked specimens between sheets of absorbent paper and then storing them under weight or pressure in dry conditions for several weeks. To retain their natural shape during the drying-out period, an even distribution of weight is important.

Book presses

This can be obtained with books, preferably ones of matching size. Old encyclopedias are perfect for this purpose and a full set is a valuable aid for the flower enthusiast! A local auction could produce a mixed assortment of books from a household, including large single volumes and books printed on matt paper. These later are always useful, regardless of size, because the absorbent paper assists the drying. Valued or valuable books should never, however, be used for plant pressing because the extra sheets of inserted storage papers will eventually weaken the spine and distort the book's shape.

Once the papers and material are placed in storage, they should remain undisturbed for a minimum period of six weeks.

Depending on depth, several sets of plant material can be stored in one book, providing sufficient pages are left between each set to leave a smooth, level surface; but it is important not to overload a book to the extent that the cover cannot lie flat or the sets slope towards the centre. Apart from damaging the spine, there is the risk of the material slipping out of position. Also it is difficult to stack other books safely on top.

Cardboard presses

Books can also form the top and base of a flower press when layers of material are placed between the closed covers. A multi-layered press can be easily assembled by cutting sheets of corrugated cardboard to match the size of the book covers. You will need two sheets of card for each set of storage papers. Place one sheet of card on top of the closed base book and, if necessary, place two or three sheets of paper over the card to cover any irregularities in the surface. Place the first set of storage sheets in position, cover with more sheets

of paper and then place another two layers of card on top, taking care to keep the edges level. This stacking can be repeated so long as the pile maintains a balanced height. It is then weighted with two or three large volumes. The little tunnels in the corrugated card allow warm air to circulate through the press to speed up the drying.

If the available supply of books has been exhausted, there are other paper sources to consider. Thick disused telephone directories, mail order catalogues, magazines and newspapers can be used but it is important to flank them with firm covers. Thick paperbacks can curl at the edges, while unsupported stacks of glossy paper have a tendency to spill on to the floor. Pieces of plywood make suitable covers and inserts of corrugated card will ventilate the paper bulk. Bricks can be used as weights in place of books but they also should be evenly distributed over the surface of the top cover. With experience, collectors can devise their own version of the flower press and improvisations ranging from converted trouser presses to slats bound with rubber bands have all been found serviceable. All types of adaptations can prove successful in fact, providing the following principles of plant pressing are taken into account.

Pressing principles

1. It is essential to use *dry* pressing materials. All books, bricks, corrugated cardboard, papers, wood and printed matter should therefore be thoroughly aired in a warm dry atmosphere well before they are required for pressing. Warm kitchens exposed to clouds of steam should be avoided along with other potentially damp quarters! As a precaution, it is worthwhile running a dry iron over all the paper material to eliminate any trace of moisture which might have accumulated during storage.
2. Plants must be free of external moisture when they are picked for the press. This means that they cannot be collected on wet days or while dew is still on the ground. The safest collecting time is from midday to the afternoon on dry days, although this can be extended on fine summer days. Certain species of plant only thrive in damp, shady surroundings and these will wilt rapidly once they are removed from their habitat. Such problems are best left to the determined naturalist

A dark background highlights the finest details,
not always to the best advantage! In this
arrangement on black velvet, the colours and
delicate shapes of the petals, dried seed pods and a
bleached Pea tendril are seen clearly whilst the
tiny insect bites in the yellow Potentilla flower are
also visible. Does the nibbled flower head suggest
an amusing reminder of a wild life party or do the
imperfections form a distracting eye-sore? When
working on contrasting colours, natural flaws as
well as finery come into close focus.

unless collectors are ardent enough to juggle with petals, papers and presses while attempting to retain their balance in mud or wet grass.

3. Once a plant is picked, the dying process begins. If much of the original colour and shape is to be preserved therefore, it should be prepared and pressed immediately. Of course, this is not always possible and specimens will require careful packaging if they are to withstand a long journey.

When you are gathering some distance from home, assemble a kit consisting of a suitable carrier, a selection of containers packed with soaked cotton wool or thick domestic tissue, a plastic container of water with a screw stopper and a pair of scissors. Cut the stems close to the ground and group them in the containers according to size. Use the water to refresh the padding from time to time, taking care not to splash the plants. Once home, they can be left to stand in water in a cool area before being prepared for the press. Although this method may seem cumbersome, it is much more effective than sealing picked flower heads in plastic tubs. Apart from the bruising which occurs, moisture seeping from cut stems can spread on to the petals and render the collection useless for pressing.

4. Unless special textures are required, only a smooth surface will produce flowers and leaves fine enough to be included in an arrangement. All pressing papers which cannot be smoothed with a dry iron should be discarded, along with any cracked or damaged corrugated cardboard, for irregularities in the pressing surfaces will in time form indentations on the plant material.

5. If a press is insufficiently weighted, petals and leaves will shrivel up, while uneven weights will produce similarly unwelcome results. While matching bricks or books can be regarded as safe, household objects such as flatirons should be treated with caution. One placed on top of a small pile of books might work effectively but two should not be trusted unless they are identical.

6. Once picked, prepared and left in the press, plants should be left in peace but the impatient beginner often cannot resist checking on their progress. Each unnecessary exposure hinders the drying process while the petals can easily be dislodged whenever the covering sheet is removed. So long as they are left alone in dry surroundings, most plants will emerge from the press in crisp condition ready for putting into arrangements, but if they are continually prodded and pried upon during the drying period, they will either remain lank and lifeless or they will deteriorate within a short time of being taken out.

Travelling press

Quite often, it is the gift of a wooden screw press which awakens a person's interest in plant press-ing. This type of press has a distinct advantage over heavy books in that it is compact and easy to carry, but it also has certain drawbacks. The pressure is applied through four screws inserted through the corners of the covers and each time fresh material is added, the screws must be loosened and then replaced. This movement can, as I have pointed out, disturb the contents, and there is also the problem of pressure. Flimsy Primrose petals only require light pressure, while plumper flowers like Daisies require greater pressure. Two dissimilar plants can therefore make poor companions when accommodated within one section of a press. One solution lies in picking only one type of flower or leaf to fill the entire press so only one pressure is required. In a climate where unexpected rain may delay a return visit, this can be a successful way of capturing a particular crop which only flourishes for a brief period. An alternative lies in regarding the screw-press as temporary travelling measure reserved only for transporting material from the growing site to wherever it can be transferred into a more permanent press. Once these mixed assets are understood, the disillusioned beginner can dismiss early dismal results and start again with greater confidence.

Opposite. *An oblong frame is fitted with paint sprayed glass. A cut cardboard mount should never be used with pressed flowers.*

Absorbent papers

There are several different choices that can be made of absorbent papers for storage. Blotting paper can be purchased from stationery departments in a variety of shades and, when a book press is being used, it is worth investing in the thickest quality. Sheets measuring about 10½ × 5 inches (260 × 120mm) are a convenient size for medium and large books because the ends will protrude beyond the pages and serve as a marker. Small pieces, on the other hand, in a large book can be difficult to locate. For clarity, I prefer to store brightly coloured material against a white background, and pale or white pieces on a coloured paper, so that any flaws, such as broken edges, will stand out clearly.

To reduce expense, plain lining paper purchased from decorating departments can be used in place of blotting paper and, in emergencies, for example when presented with an unexpected bunch of flowers, plain writing or typing paper can be used for immediate pressing, although it is advisable to transfer the material to a more absorbent paper at the first opportunity. Providing the paper is plain and clean it will be serviceable, but

remember, *never* use printed paper. The inks will discolour the material.

Soft domestic tissue is a useful drying agent but the material should not be placed against folds or perforations. With bulky material, tissue can be used as padding between the plants and the papers, and the final results are often worth the extra trouble of cushioning in this manner. Only use plain toilet paper for this purpose, however; thick kitchen tissue is ideal for a further purpose.

Most household tissues have a pattern embossed on the surface. This fact had escaped my notice until one day when I opened a set of Hydrangea florets and found that each petal was stamped with a pattern of tiny dots. These were removed to a press reserved for oddments and I did not bother to look at them until many months later when I was experimenting with figures dressed in period costume. The petals then proved perfect for representing the textured surface of fabric — so that while kitchen paper is totally unsuitable for preserving natural forms, it can be fun to use it for embossing different petal surfaces.

CHAPTER TWO
Specimens and sources

CHAPTER TWO

Specimens and sources

My first plant pressings were gathered from a city centre but, in my eagerness to collect as many specimens as possible, I did not make a note of my local discoveries. This resulted in a great deal of frustration when I went in search of further supplies the following year. On a stretch of waste land near a railway station I had come across a small gathering of pink flowers accompanied by magnificent spiked rust leaves, which I subsequently identified as a species of Cranesbill. Although I was familiar with the general layout, I could not locate the exact place again until the crop had almost died away and only a few withered leaves remained. Another misadventure arose with a track of Herb Robert which sprawled along a tarmac path. This time I had no trouble in locating the plants again but I returned too late in the year, by which time the leaves were large and dark, missing the tiny growths with their brilliant pink colours. A textbook on plant life will give you a general guide on where certain species can be found and their flowering periods, but nature does not always follow a strict pattern.

Selecting material

Varying weather conditions can delay or encourage growth in a particular area, and of course, plants in shadowed positions seldom grow at the same pace as their sun-sited companions. In order to pick the earliest growths and smallest specimens while they are still in a suitable condition for pressing, the collector must be prepared to revisit a potential site at regular intervals. Even a delay of a fortnight can deprive you of a favourite selection of material until it reappears the following year. Since I have missed several crops through neglecting to keep a simple record, I strongly advise any collector to take a note of his or her local discoveries, the exact site on which they were found and the date on which they were picked.

Another mistake of mine was failing to keep a scrap book of specimens because, along with the many delights in store for the collector, there are inevitably also a few disappointments. Some flowers do not retain their original colours when dried, particularly the blue range of wild plants. Notable exceptions are Larkspur and Delphinium, both garden flowers which can be regarded as the permanent blues of the floral palette. Reds

often acquire a brownish tinge when dried, bright greenery is apt to lose its fresh tint, pinks and purples can fade into muted beiges and grey tones. Orange and yellow flowers usually show the best colour retention and, while some white flowers remain surprisingly fresh, others turn to a dingy shade of brown. It is useful to keep a scrap book in which to record such changes, along with samples of pressings, and for anyone with only limited space, it is a helpful guide especially when only the most worthwhile material is accommodated. With a little ingenuity and imagination, faded specimens can be shown to subtle advantage when used in a suitable arrangement, but the problems in plant pressings can be minimised if an unknown plant is closely examined for tell-tale features which provide clues to its qualities when pressed.

Plant material

Pick a flower head and closely examine its construction. Do the petals join into a tube at the base? If so, it will probably be easy to prepare for pressing. Or does the flower head consist of separate petals held together by a calyx or green particles at the base? Gently press into the centre of the flower to see if the petals fold back easily and remain joined to the base. If the flower disintegrates, it will not stand up to the strain of pressing in the open position but it might be suitable for pressing in the sideway position.

Pick another flower head from the same group and gently press the petals together in a closed position. Exert extra pressure on the calyx with a slight pinch. If the petals remain intact, it will be suitable for pressing in the sideway position. The pale pink and mauve petals of the Lady's Smock or Cuckoo Flower can only be pressed in this position or individually. (See Figures 3,3A). Once the potential strength has been assessed, there are other questions to consider. Are the petals thin and open, or fleshy and close together? Petals like those of the Potentilla will press successfully but if moisture seeps out from a fleshy flower when crushed between the fingertips, it may be difficult to dry out. Bluebells fall within this category and while some arrangers recommend cutting bell shapes into two halves to lessen the bulk, the results are inclined to look strained and unnatural. An easier solution lies in pressing more suitable bell shapes like those which flower on the

A bowl of flowers displayed on a burgundy base
*A large Hydrangea petal is trimmed down to form
a bowl that contains an assortment of flowers.
The rust leaf of a Cut-leaved Cranesbill and a
single Forget-me-not head are positioned to hide
the straight scissor cut line which could disturb
the natural presentation. Single florets and flowers
lightly extend the arrangement towards the edge
of the frame, while two green coiling Pea tendrils
and a cluster of Cow Parsley hold the
arrangement down towards the base.*

pink and red Heuchera plants. The dried colour of a flower is sometimes difficult to assess in advance but a wilting flower may give an indication of the final result. If some of the petals have wilted in beige or coffee shades, it is unlikely to retain its original colour but if the shape is attractive you might decide the material is worth preserving. The delicate colours of the Pea flowers often fade away completely but the dried creamy white petals can be overlapped to form full multi-layered flower shapes which cannot be obtained by other means, like the central flower on the pink pot lid shown on page 57.

Sometimes the frailest of petals are accompanied by large lumpy stigmas in the centres and if these cannot be removed, the petals will shrivel up because they cannot lie flat within the press. When placed in the open or sideway position, do pieces protrude which cannot be plucked away? If so, the complete head is unsuitable for pressing and you will need to decide if the petals are worth pressing individually. Finally, are the flowers in healthy condition and do the selected pressing shapes look attractive? If a flower has to be pruned or forced too much out of its natural shape in the attempt to press it, the result may be awkward and far from appealing. Insects can damage fragile petals, flowers can be snagged by brittle neighbours and scorched or bruised by weather conditions. For some curious reason there are certain flower pressers who are under the impression that blemishes will mysteriously vanish within the press while the opposite occurs. A withered petal or tattered edge may escape detection amongst living plants but once pressed, these flaws will stand out clearly. Like ladies who are subject to good and bad days, flowers also have their off-peak periods and there is little point in picking those which are reluctant to come out or who are downright dowdy around the edges. With a little effort beautiful specimens can be sorted from those which are far from perfect and while commercial arrangers often seem content to use material which is second-rate, miniature artists should reserve their skill and patience for the finest materials.

Selection list of Miniature material

At present, I have several unfamiliar plants in the process of being pressed and until the time comes to examine them, I will not know whether they have dried successfully. Each year I try to collect large quantities of the material which I know will dry well and prove useful in arrangements, but I also reserve room for a few strangers for experimental purposes. A collector's list of recommended plants must therefore remain incomplete but, for the beginner, here is a short selection of Miniature material and the sources where it can be easily obtained in most areas.

Name	Location	Part for pressing
Alyssum	From seed or garden nurseries	Flowers
Aquilegia (Columbine)	Garden nurseries, sometimes wild	Leaves
Broom	Commons, wastelands	Flowers
Buttercup	Grass banks, fields, wastelands	Flowers
Candytuft	From seed	Flowers and leaves
Cleavers (Goosegrass)	Hedges, fences, wastelands	Leaves
Clover	Grass verges, banks	Flowers and leaves
Cow Parsley	Roadsides, ditches, wastelands	Floret clusters
Cowslips (Cultivated)	From seed or garden nurseries	Flowers, calyx, stems

Name	Location	Part for pressing
Curly Chevril	Herb bed, garden nurseries	Cream leaves
Cut-leaved Cranesbill	Grass lands, wastelands	Rust, spiked leaves
Daisy (Lawn)	Lawns, grass lands, wastelands	Flowers
Delphinium	Garden nurseries, florist	Florets
Fat Hen Dock	Waysides, wastelands	Flowers
Ferns	Woods, walls, florist	Leaves
Forget-me-not	From seed, garden nurseries, stream banks	Flowers and sprigs
Geums	Garden nurseries	Flowers, rust leaves
Gold Dust	Garden nurseries	Flowers
Gorse	Heaths, wastelands	Flowers
Grasses	Road sides, wastelands	Bleached tips
Ground ivies	Hedges, undergrowth, wastelands	Flowers, small leaves
Heather	Moors, garden nurseries	Flowers
Herb Robert	Hedgerows, verges, tracks	Leaves
Heuchera	Garden nurseries	Flowers
Hop Trefoil	Grass verges, meadows	Flowers and stems
Iberis	From seed, garden nurseries	Flowers
Ivy	Brickwork, woods, florist	Leaves
Ivy-leaved Toadflax	Brick and stonework, walls	Leaves, stems and flowers
Lady's Smock	Meadows	Flowers
Larkspur	From seed, garden nurseries, florist	Florets
Lesser Celandine	Grass banks, roadsides, hedges	Flowers
Lobelia	From seed, garden nurseries	Flowers
Melilot	Wastelands, fields, hedges	Flowers
Montbretia	Garden nurseries, florist	Flowers
Moss	Brickwork, woods, florist	Strands
Nettles	Roadsides, wastelands	Flowers, small leaves
Pansy (Dwarf)	From seed, garden nurseries	Flowers
Peas	Vegetable plot, grass banks	Tendrils
Periwinkle	From seed, shaded areas, wood banks	Flowers
Polyanthus	From garden nurseries	Flowers, calyx and stems
Potentilla	Shrub, garden nurseries	Flowers and leaves
Primroses	Woodlands, banks, roadsides	Flowers, calyx and stems
Red Valerian	Railway banks, stone walls	Flowers
Rock Roses	Rockery, garden nurseries	Flowers
Rosebay Willowherb	Wastelands, roadsides	Florets
Scarlet Pimpernel	Garden weed, wastelands	Flowers, stems and leaves
Sorrel (Common)	Meadows, wastelands	Flowers
Speedwell	Banks, fields, wastelands	Flowers, stems and leaves
Sweet Peas	From garden nurseries	Flowers and tendrils
Verbena	From garden nurseries	Flowers
Vetch (All varieties)	Grass banks, meadows	Flowers and tendrils
Wild Pansy	Hills, pasture, wastelands	Flowers

If you extend your search into the countryside for wild plants, it is important to remember that some species are in danger of becoming extinct. In 1981 the Wildlife and Countryside Act expanded the list of protected plants and made it illegal to pick any of the species listed on page 91 at the back of this book. It is also illegal to uproot any wild plant without the landowner's consent and because it is essential that flowers should be left to seed if they are to survive, I have recommended cultivated Cowslips from a nursery instead of the wild variety. Packets of wild plant seed can now be purchased and these should be sown and raised whenever possible in order to conserve our countryside. Because you will only need small quantities of flowers, there is little harm in picking a few Primroses; but never remove all the flower heads from one plant because it is this form of careless collecting which will in time eliminate an entire species.

Leaves, stems and tendrils

With a beautiful selection of colourful flowers demanding our immediate attention, it is easy to overlook the important role played in arrangements by leaves and stems.

Very often, the flower head will form the main focal point of colour but leaves and stems add the delicate balance and movement to a design. For each flower you may need two or three leaves, so press a wide selection in sufficient quantities. Curling stems are particularly useful; these should also be collected in large numbers, along with other coiling and curving shapes. Pea tendrils supply beautiful details and, apart from pressing plenty of green ones, I make a stock of pale ones by boiling them in water with a small quantity of domestic bleach. When they have turned to a creamy colour, I pour them into a fine strainer and rinse them under cold water before leaving them to dry out on a piece of blotting paper. Dandelion clocks and Thistledowns, along with tiny dried seed pods, are a valuable source of detail and these should be collected and stored in tied paper bags.

After you have been collecting for a full season, you will notice that some plants only appear for a very short time while others flourish for several weeks. Always take the first opportunity to gather in those which are inclined to vanish quickly when they appear the following year and leave the long stayers until a later date. While you might wait for twelve months for their arrival, you will find some who are not prepared to wait a week for you.

CHAPTER THREE
Preparing plants for the press

Preparing plants for the press

At one time or another, you might have casually picked and pressed a flower inside a book only to have forgotten about it until a much later date. If the result was a smooth, well-defined specimen, luck probably played a large part because most unprepared pressings emerge in confused clumps of unrecognizable plant matter. This is caused through the different thicknesses contained in various parts of one plant. In order to obtain flowers and leaves suitable for arrangements, it is necessary to separate the plants into sections and eliminate surplus bulk wherever possible. With the exception of very small plants like Scarlet Pimpernel or Speedwell, the stalks should be removed from flower heads and the temptation to press a mixed selection together should always be resisted because the slightest variation in thickness will greatly increase the risk of distortion through shrinkage and shrivelling. In many instances, only one part of a plant is required and to avoid wasting valuable storage space, it is sensible to prepare sufficient material to cover one sheet of storage paper.

As your collection increases, you will notice several basic variations in flower head construction and the following guide will help you to prepare some of the main types in a suitable manner.

Cups and saucers (Figs. 1, 1a)

Primroses along with many other saucer-shaped flowers have petals which join into a tube at the base. To enable a head to open out flat, it is necessary to remove the tube by snipping it away with a small pair of sharp scissors. Although hardly visible at the time, petals can be bruised by heavy handling so, whenever possible, hold a plant by the stem with the head facing downwards over the sheet of paper selected for storage. If possible, trim so that the head falls directly on to the sheet facing downwards.

When a sufficient quantity has been prepared, space them apart with a needle inserted through the small hole in the centre. Flower petals should never overlap, and because they will take up more space when pressed flat it is worth leaving a little more space between them than seems strictly necessary.

When pressing cup or saucer shapes in the sideway position, leave the tube in place. These can be trimmed away once the flower has dried. Some arrangers use a two-thirds position by placing a head in the sideway position and then folding back a portion of the upper petals, but the straight line which is folded through the centre is inclined to look unnatural, especially on larger flowers.

Fig. 1

Fig. 1a

Cutting down to size
In their original condition, some of the flowers shown in these small pendants would have been too large or too poor in quality for miniature presentation. Careful plucking can extend the range of material or display it in a different manner.

Top. *A yellow spray is completed with two single Melilot florets taken from the top of the flower head.*
Right. *The shrivelled petals of a poorly pressed Buttercup are removed to reveal the bright stamens in the centre.*
Left. *The outer petals of a pink Candytuft are picked out to leave a small, well-defined flower head.*

Flutes and trumpets *(Figs. 2, 2a, 3, 3a)*

Nettles, Ground Ivies and some species of wild Orchid have tubular-based trumpet flowers which can be coaxed from their bracts by careful handling. When pressed sideways, the fluted lips will form elegant trumpet shapes but, when pressed facing upwards, they are inclined to look squat and somewhat squashed. Small shapes like these should be arranged in rows facing in one direction with the top of the flowers pointing towards the upper edge of the storage sheet. The covering sheet can then be applied so that it rolls from the base to the top of the petals, helping to smooth out potential puckers and creases. The same layout should be used for rows of single petals, for flowers with separated petals placed in the sideway position, and for leaves.

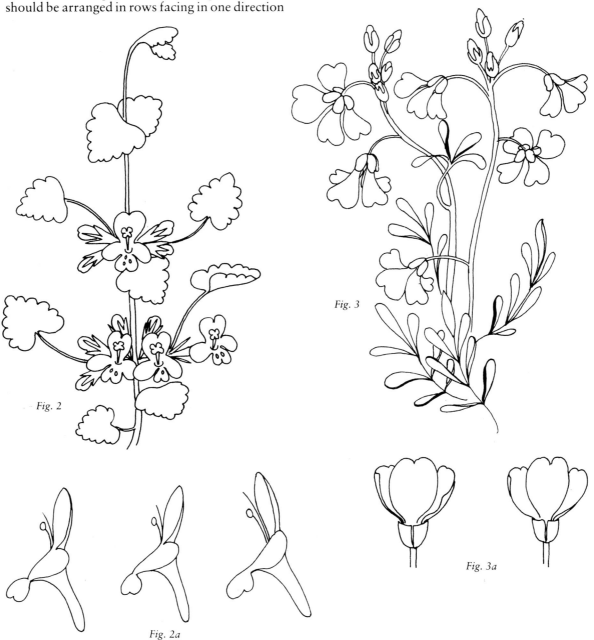

Fig. 2

Fig. 3

Fig. 2a

Fig. 3a

Floret fillings. *Not all flowers have delicate outlines and these pink Hydrangea heads, with their angular petals, are one example.*

This arrangement shows how floret clusters can be used to soften the blunt edges without concealing the underlying colours, and they are also useful for lightly linking pieces together in a border spray or for filling in awkward gaps. The neutral white of Cow Parsley is particularly convenient for fillings and bridge-work. Clusters of pink Alyssum and Gold Dust are also suitable fillers although their colours must be taken into consideration in the general scheme.

To complete this arrangement, should yellow be introduced into the basically pink theme of Hydrangeas, Alyssum and Heuchera flowers?

Above. *Warm rusts contrast against cool creams on a dark brown background to create a suggestion of autumn. The tips of bleached grass form the main lines of the sweeping spray and, to continue the circular shape, Heuchera flowers have been spaced around the base below the Iberis flower.*

Subdued tones can often be enhanced with sparing touches of bright colour. By covering up the pink and blue flowers in the arrangement on page 29, the remaining shades may appear rather dull in comparison or, alternatively, the basic autumnal colouring may look more harmonious without the flower tints. While the final decision lies with the miniaturist, it is technically advisable to secure the main shapes and leave the finishing touches free for last-minute removals or rearrangements.

Opposite. *Deep blue velvet displays dried seed heads and a faded cluster of gold dust with rust strands of Common Sorrel. Pink Clover flowers and a Nettle flute complete the leaf base on the left-hand side.*

Pot bellies (Figs. 4, 4a)

The Common Lawn Daisy with its plump raised centre often looks disappointingly straggly when pressed, but when it is treated with a very firm hand, it responds surprisingly well.

Because Daisies grow in great abundance, it is easy to pick too many at one time and, quite often, too little attention is given to the condition of the flower. Do not be fooled into thinking that one Daisy is very much the same as the next because, if you look closely, you will find some which look full and firm while others appear to have been on a diet.

Only pick a few of the plumpest ones, remove the stalks and place them face downwards on the paper. Press down each base very firmly with the thumb to flatten out the centres, cover as quickly as possible and store under extra heavy weight, such as under a pile of books. The Buttercup with its bulbous centre should also be treated in the same heavy-handed manner because the petals will swiftly shrivel up if prepared in a timid fashion.

Bush heads (Figs. 5, 5a)

Some flowers, like Alyssum or Gold Dust, have a bushy head which extends down the stalk with growth and do not have a distinctive part, such as a bract, to serve as a cutting guide. These should be held head downwards above the paper and snipped across the stem just below the fullest spread of petals or before the petals start to thin out. With pyramid shapes, snip off the points and press these together in one set of paper. Trim the remaining lengths of stalks with petals into thin slices to use as flower wheels or particles if they are misshapen.

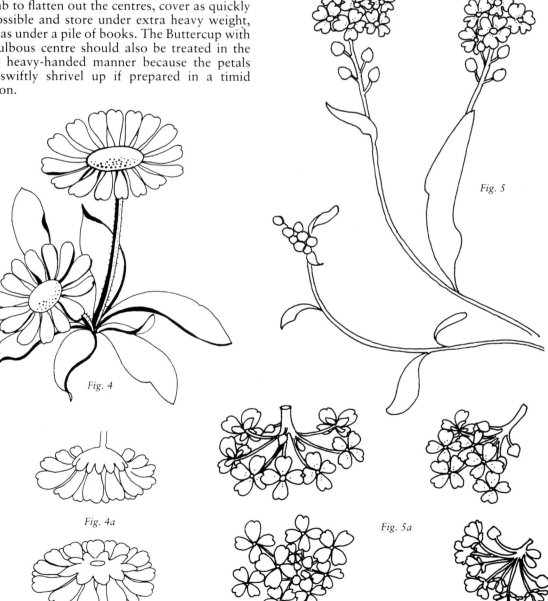

Fig. 4

Fig. 4a

Fig. 5

Fig. 5a

Creative licence

The natural curves in this arrangement are supplied by the Scarlet Pimpernel stems, slyly extended with a tip of fern leaf and a spray of Fennel, a coiling tendril and a small sprig of Forget-me-not. The pale blue curve just above the pale green strand of moss is slightly suspect for, to balance the blues, it was sliced from a Delphinium petal.

Other dubious shapes include the single pink petal added to strengthen the colour of the Scarlet Pimpernels along with an Alyssum floret, while a pink Candytuft floret plucked from the main head serves the same purpose on the lower right-hand side. Beyond all belief, there is the pink and yellow flower which was manufactured to extend the pink tones and the yellow florets of Gold Dust. Unlike the naturalist restricted to accurate detail, the miniaturist is free to choose, cut, and compile whenever necessary. And cheat!

Clusters (Figs. 6, 6a)

Various types of hedgerow parsley thrive on the roadside. From a distant glance, it is difficult to distinguish them from Wild Carrot and Hemlock because they all bear clusters of white florets.

Cow Parsley, often called Queen Anne's Lace, is a suitable pressing variety because the thin bracteoles at the base of each cluster easily open out and allow the florets to lie flat. Cut the smallest clusters from their stalks just below the bracteoles and arrange them facing downwards on the paper. Before covering, press down each base in order to spread the florets to their fullest extent because these clusters can take up a surprising amount of space.

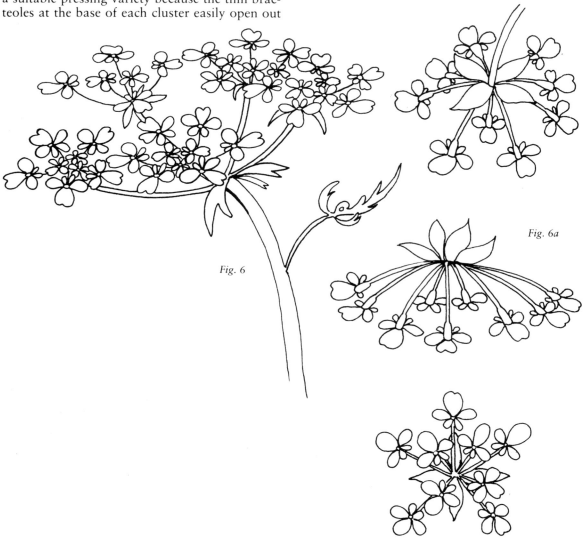

Fig. 6

Fig. 6a

32

Top left. *The lower tip of a Daisy spray is finished with bleached grass and a seed pod with two Candytuft florets.*

Top centre. *A circular spray is completed with single Cow Parsley florets falling from a pink Nettle flute.*

Top right. *A rust and yellow arrangement with a curved piece of trimmed ribbon cut from a Carnation petal.*

Below left. *Two Vetch flowers and a yellow Melilot tip curve towards an Aquilegia leaf.*

Below centre. *Bleached colours and dried heads with a soft golden centre of Broom flowers.*

Below right. *A pink Larkspur flower trimmed to look in one direction faces towards the centre of the frame, not away from the edge.*

Multi-layers *(Figs. 7, 7a)*

Flowers which have several layers of petals can be successfully pressed, although their bulk will have to be lessened by plucking out some of the petals. This requires a certain amount of skill and judgement because, if too many petals are removed, the head will disintegrate into a shower of separate petals. After varying results, I now prefer to remove only the minimum number of petals before pressing under extra weight, and I leave the final trimming until the material has dried out. Creased petals can be removed from the front and the shape is often more delicate and clearly defined after the larger petals have been plucked from the back.

Although curly and full, the double florets of Delphiniums dry surprisingly well. Snip the florets from the stalk and arrange facing downwards, pressing down the protruding spurs with your fingertip before covering. A full floret is often too large for a small arrangement but one will supply many lovely petals which can be used individually and it is worth searching for the Black Eye varieties which are extremely beautiful. The Larkspur can also be prepared in the same manner.

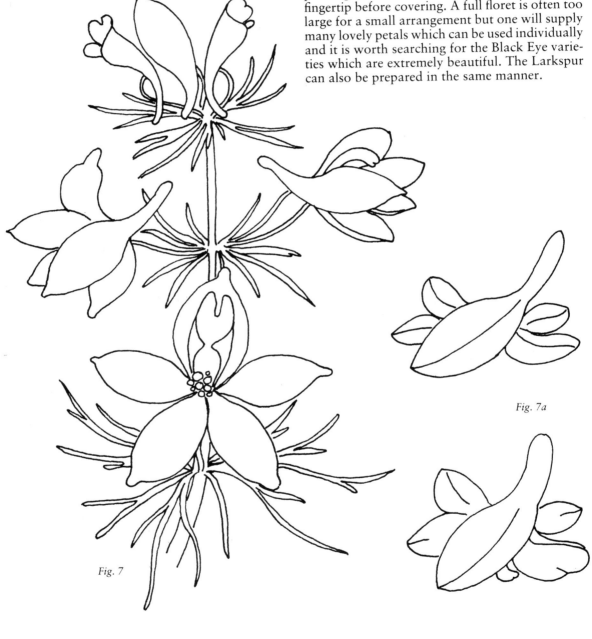

Fig. 7a

Fig. 7

A mounted miniature. *An arrangement containing a white Iberis flower, flanked with leaves of sun-bleached Fool's Parsley and green Aquiligea leaves, receives extra emphasis in a mounted presentation.*

Conventional methods of mounting can seldom be used with pressed flowers because the work must be sealed securely from moisture for, all too often, a complex piece of work is destroyed through inadequate protection. For the details, see chapter five, page 78.

Singles and sprays (Figs. 8, 8a)

Some plants have flowers which are suitable for pressing in spray form, or individually; and one of the best examples is the Forget-me-not with its tiny saucer-shaped flowers and curving branches. Although the handling of petals is best generally avoided, a slight squeeze on some of the partially opened buds will help to define the pressing shape. Position the sprigs with the fully opened flowers facing upwards and the buds resting sideways. Even when these pressings are not entirely successful, the small curls of closed buds can be retained for detail. Fully opened flower heads can be snipped directly on to the storage sheet of paper and separated into place with a needle.

Because these little flowers are so suitable for miniature work, it is worth preparing them in large quantities. By placing the plants in water on a sunny window ledge after the first crop of opened heads has been gathered, the buds will open out to provide further supplies. Speedwell and Scarlet Pimpernel are also two-way pressers but because their petals are so flimsy, they are easier to press sideways.

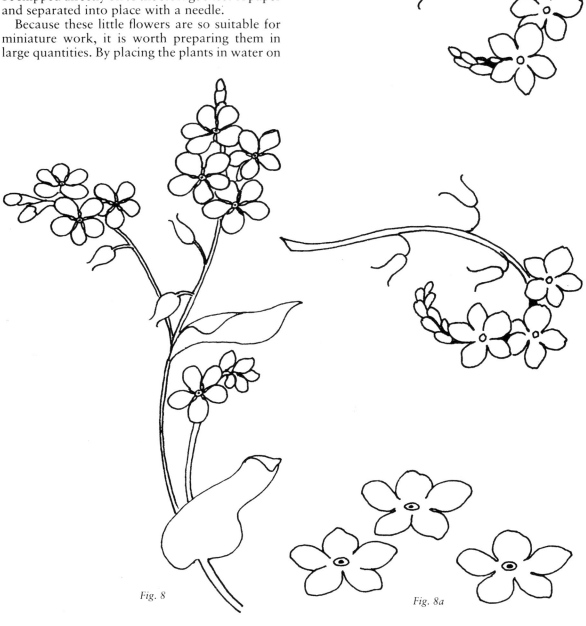

Fig. 8

Fig. 8a

A selection of jewellery fittings

Top. *An old-fashioned oval brooch is restored with a cream satin lining and a new perspex cover. Tiny stems of Ivy-leaved Toadflax are used to support Forget-me-not heads and pink Alyssum florets.*

Below. *A silk-lined pendant shows a flimsy pink flower firmly secured in the centre with a single Forget-me-not head.*

Right. *Two watch glasses are glued together to make a pendant which contains an arrangement on each side. The work is suspended in a silver mount designed to hold a crown piece.*

Left. *A pendant is lined with a piece of shot-silk cut from a Tulip petal.*

Spikes and spears *(Figs. 9, 9a)*

Tall, spikey plants like Common Sorrel and Melilot should be cut into strands of convenient length for the press and if they are stiff and bulky, they should be padded with layers of thin absorbent tissue. The tips with the smallest flowers can be used in arrangements while the lengths with the blunt cut tips are only suitable for supplying particles.

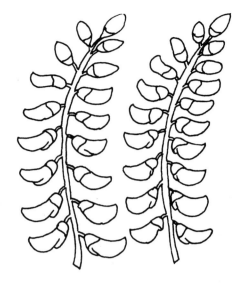

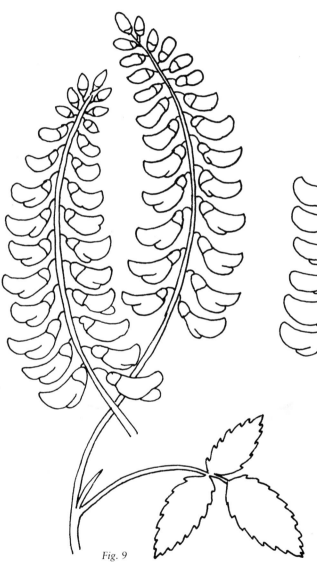

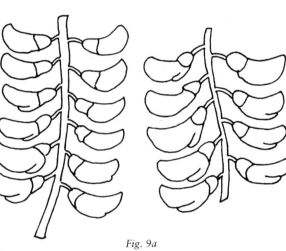

Fig. 9a

Fig. 9

Scaling down

Once familiar with miniature work, the tiny size of these pots and pill containers will provide an amusing challenge for the arranger.

Top left. A Potentilla flower on a blue Delphinium base is surrounded with pink Alyssum florets.

Top right. A garland arrangement surrounds a Cranesbill leaf.

Centre. Scarlet Pimpernels spray from a trimmed rust leaf.

Bottom left. Small, smaller and the smallest Forget-me-not heads!

Bottom right. The lower tip of the spray is completed with a single star of Common Sorrel. The upper tip is finished with a fragment of grass, Curly Chevril and a dried Shepherd's Purse pod.

Curlers (Figs. 10, 10a)

Dwarf Pansies, and members of the Viola family, can be difficult to control because their petals have a tendency to curl up as soon as they are picked. Only pick a few at one time, therefore, and leave a small length of stalk attached to each head because the irregular petals will fall apart if trimmed too closely.

Place them facing downwards with the larger upper petals pointing towards the top of the storage sheet. Press down the protruding spurs with the fingertip and roll the covering sheet first into position over the lower petals. If this is done speedily, these elusive flower faces can be successfully captured.

The bright Rosebay Willowherb is also inclined to droop within minutes of picking and one plant with several open florets is usually ample for one pressing. Cut the florets beneath the purple pointed base and arrange face downwards on the paper. Even when the petals fail to press well, the dark sepals provide interesting shapes.

Fig. 10a

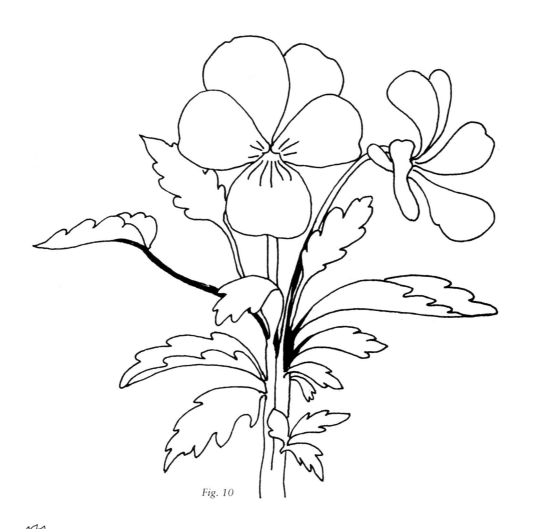

Fig. 10

Changing complexions
A mauve Pansy changes her original complexion for a flattering colour of palest cream!

Against a white background, this subtle transformation would be lost while the colour balance could also be disturbed with the eventual loss of the central tint. When working with fast faders, use a contrasting background so that the shapes can be fully appreciated long after the colours have departed. In anticipation of the change of colour, a light Curly Chevril leaf has been positioned to extend the Pansy shape towards the base.

Fat heads *(Figs. 11, 11a)*

Thick Clover heads should be split into segments and pressed under extra weight while the smaller clover shaped flowers like the yellow Hop Trefoil and Black Medick can be pressed complete with a short amount of stalk.

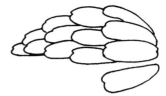

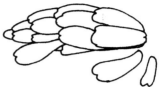

Fig. 11a

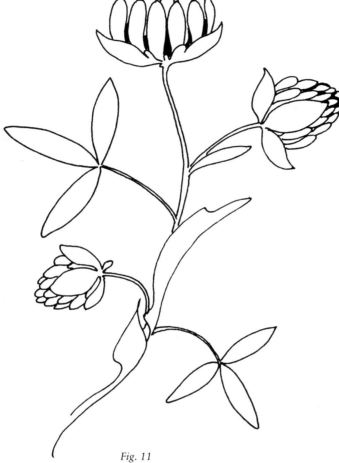

Fig. 11

Free-floating forms

These abstract compositions consist of overlapping petals which allow the underlying colours and shapes to merge into subtle shades. Apart from making good use of petals which are generally unsuitable – because they are too large, misshapen, flimsy or faded – they also offer a different form of art work. Success depends on the swirling balance of colour and the floating impression of petals.

On closer examination, these abstracts are not so simple to construct as might appear at first glance. Adhesive, for example, can only be applied around the outer edge of the base where it will be concealed by the frame, not inside the central area.

Left. *Yellow Carnation petals lap against the black-tipped petals of Delphinium.*

Right. *Pink Geranium petals in fanned and folded positions form orange tones over a yellow Primrose base. Overlaid Delphiniums produce shades of slate-blue with a Candytuft floret supplying the splash of bright pink.*

Preparing the plants

Before preparing the plants, place the lower sheet of blotting paper on the page of the opened book in which it is to be stored or on the cardboard sheet of a multi-layered press. This will prevent unnecessary movement of the material afterwards. When the plant pieces have been prepared and spaced apart correctly, the upper sheet should be lowered into position very slowly because swift movement can disturb all your careful preparation. With flowers which have been positioned to face in one direction, as described on page 26, match the two bottom edges of the paper exactly and gently roll or bend the top sheet in place while keeping the sides level. If the pieces have been simply spaced apart, slowly lower the upper sheet directly down over the material.

On a strip of paper, clearly mark the name of the stored pieces and the date on which they were pressed. Place this beside the set so that the information protrudes from the page. Sometimes, when I was in a hurry, I neglected to do this at the time with the intention of marking the contents later. It is a mistake, especially when using encyclopaedias matching in shape, size and colour, and for the saved two or three minutes I have in the long run wasted hours.

CHAPTER FOUR
Arrangements

Arrangements

Assembling dried material

While some people seem to possess a natural talent for artistic arrangements, others have to acquire the skill by simple stages. Achieving a graceful design with dried plant material often requires a certain amount of practice, especially when working for the first time on a small scale. To avoid spoiling good miniature bases with early experiments, mark out the shape and size of the base several times on scrap paper and when a frame is to be added, clearly mark where the inner edge of the frame will lie inside the base. This will give an accurate idea of the available space because it is easy to over-estimate the size of the working surface.

Select various pieces of dried material and place them inside the marked areas in order to gain a correct idea of their size. Very often, a small leaf or flower will seem surprisingly large when first encircled within the miniature area.

Individual pieces of material can be transported on a needle steadied with the index finger; the tweezers used by many arrangers are often too large for the little pieces although they can be used for handling larger shapes. Continue to experiment with different pieces of plant matter until you become familiar with the shapes, sizes and the surrounding space. A successful arrangement should be neatly contained within the framed area, with sufficient space to show detail to the best advantage. A common mistake is over-crowding, with too many pieces, or making the arrangement too large, resulting in visual confusion or ugly broken blunt edges when the arrangement is cut off by the frame.

Whenever possible, always aim for uniform thickness in dried material, particularly when using plastic film as a covering. Thin petals can be overlapped or superimposed, but frail material should never be placed over bulky pieces, such as a stiff stalk, because it will crack or crease when the protective covering is eventually pressed firmly into place. Stalks and leaves can be trimmed at the base with scissors to meet the edge of delicate petals; a tapered or diagonal cut will look more elegant than a blunt straight snip.

Plant material can be secured into position with light applications of adhesive suitable for paper, and this can be purchased in tube or pencil form from stationery departments. Once fixed, dried material should not be moved; brittle pieces are liable to snap and exposed spots of adhesive will discolour in time. Always arrange the main pieces in a harmonious, basic design prior to fixing so that the shapes and colours can be adjusted when necessary. If a piece of fixed material must be removed, lift it up with a needle and scrape away all trace of the adhesive with a fine point. A paper surface will probably show scratch marks but these can often be disguised by covering with another piece of material.

Adhesive techniques

Depending on the size and shape to be secured, adhesive can be applied in two ways. With a larger piece, such as a fully opened flower head or leaf, a speck of adhesive can be removed directly from the container with the point of a needle and lightly spread on to the surface of the background. The piece can then be placed on top and lightly pressed down with the fingertip. If the piece is very tiny, lift it up on a needle point and place a minute speck underneath it before positioning it in the arrangement. After a certain amount of practice, you will learn where to place adhesive specks so they cannot be seen, or, alternatively, how to disguise them. A group of slender particles, such as a stemmed Scarlet Pimpernel, a strand of moss and a seed pod can be secured at their bases with one speck of adhesive which can then be covered by a tiny flower like a single Forget-me-not head. Whenever possible, avoid spreading adhesive under stems or flower heads if they can be secured at the base because they will lie in a more natural position when fixed in this manner.

During the early stages, the beginner may frequently be faced with the problem of applying adhesive too scantily, so that the arrangement easily becomes dislodged, or of applying too much so that it seeps out on the base when the material is pressed into place. Certain types of adhesive also become thick and lumpy when exposed to the atmosphere for a time: these should be discarded because the adhesive cannot be spread smoothly and the bumps will become apparent under flimsy material. A few trial runs with some inferior specimens on scrap paper will help you to become familiar with the fixing technique. It will also save a great deal of irritation when it comes to assembling your first miniatures.

Sweet differences
A compact lid shows the reconstruction of Sweet William flowers in the centre. Because of the calyx construction, each petal has to be pressed separately and great care must be taken to match them when the head is reassembled if the identity of the flower is to be preserved.

To the untrained eye, one flower may look much the same as the next but the miniaturist will swiftly realise how nature does not run a smooth reproduction line. By comparing the size, shape, shade and markings of the small incomplete flower at the top, the differences become clear but the two darker flowers only vary in size. These individual characteristics can be a revelation; for the arranger, however, they can also cause headaches!

Working conditions

If there happens to be a spare room available for your assembling sessions, book it and hang a bold "Keep Out" sign outside the door because there are few occupations more precarious than handling feather light pieces of dried material. Once you start work, it will be necessary to uncover several sheets of stored material in order to select suitable shapes and colours and the slightest rush of air – from a sudden movement to a small sneeze – will be sufficient to scatter your specimens all over the place. A swiftly opened door will have the force of a hurricane and a gust of breeze through a window will assume gale strength. If an invasion of the workroom is unavoidable, insist that all who enter approach with the speed of a weary snail. Even in isolation, however, your material might not be safe. An unexpected cough has scattered an arrangement which has taken me hours to prepare and carefully positioned particles have been brushed out of place when I have forgotten to pin back my hair.

Whenever possible, work on a large table in front of a closed window by natural daylight or use an adjustable angle lamp for extra light. In deep concentration it is easy to continue working without noticing the change of light and it is a mistake to work in the shadows cast by your hands or shoulders. Work which looks competent in such conditions often looks shoddy when reviewed in daylight.

Because the time factor cannot be completely ignored when working with exposed dried material, I like to prepare with a full pack of needles and a pin cushion, two sources of adhesive, a saucer and a couple of pairs of small scissors so that time is not wasted by searching. Neat workers will probably manage to wipe needles clear of adhesive with a sheet of tissue, but for the less methodical I recommend a piece of old sheeting to be used as a cover over the working surface. All blobs of adhesive can be wiped on to the edge and you will have the advantage of knowing exactly where they are. Tacky tissue can easily catch on clothing and, once the adhesive smears, it is not difficult to emerge after a session with a fancy outfit decked with stray petals!

Whenever possible, aim to complete one miniature during one session, including the sealing and framing, because the material cannot be left uncovered especially in a room which is only used occasionally. It will soon become limp and useless or curl up around the edges. Dried material should be stored in conditions similiar to those used for pressing: a stack with inserted sheets of corrugated cardboard is a convenient method. It is inadvisable to store pieces in envelopes because the brittle material will snap into fragments should they rub together. After a while, you will amass an assortment of particles, loose petals and oddments and these should be stored together in a set and clearly marked. This mixed pack will prove extremely useful when searching for tiny finishing touches with which to complete an arrangement.

A selection of arrangements

Until you become accustomed to handling material with confidence, it is best to restrict your first arrangements to a few well-chosen pieces. Once the various methods of securing the pieces have been mastered, you will be able to create an infinite variety of original work. The following arrangements are just a few suggestions from the potential range.

Leaf swags *(Figs. 12, 12a, 12b)*

Providing each thickness is correctly positioned, leaves can be overlapped into graceful swags to form an elegant base for flower heads. To make a simple swag, select one well-defined leaf with a straight central vein, like an Ivy, and two curving leaves. When using two leaves which point in the same direction it might be necessary to turn one upside down in order to continue the line of the curve. Space the two curved leaves slightly apart to form an arc, and place the straight leaf in the centre so that it just covers the bottoms of the leaves. Adjust the leaves until they form a balanced swag, then carefully remove the central leaf so the outer leaves can be secured at their bases with adhesive. Replace the central leaf and secure with adhesive.

Longer and more elaborate swags can be assembled with the addition of more curving leaves but always position the frailest varieties at the outer tips and overlap towards the centre with firmer specimens. Details like Pea tendrils, seed pods, Nettle, and Clover flowers or moss strands can be worked into these arrangements, but care should be taken not to place them too close to the outer edge of the base because these may be stretched slightly out of position when the miniature is covered and framed.

Flower borders *(Figs. 13, 13a)*

Delicate borders of flowers, leaves and particles, which consist of small separate groups, will form an attractive arrangement and, at the same time, will teach you the basic technique of assembling plant material and how to hide the adhesive successfully. In Figure 13 the finer details are fixed into place with specks of adhesive, and in Figure 13a, these have been covered with other pieces of

Fig. 12

Fig. 12a

Fig. 12b

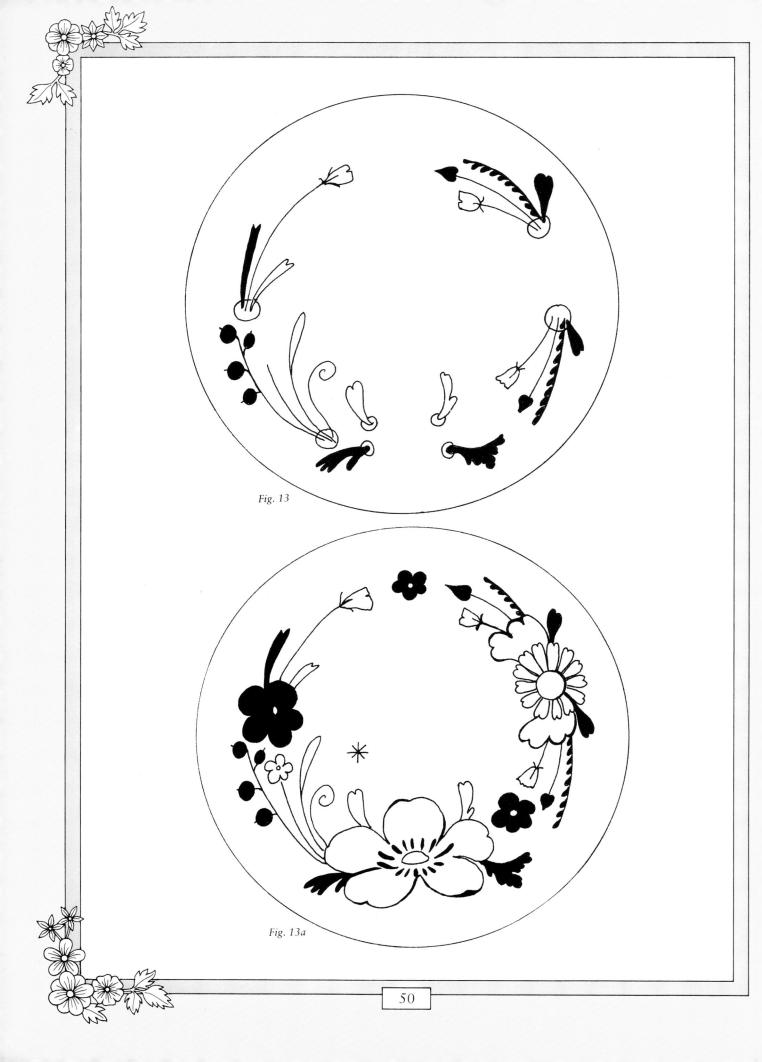

Fig. 13

Fig. 13a

A pot lid fitted with pink card makes a suitable base for learning the techniques of adhesive application. Card does offer a slight grip, while slippery fabrics such as satin require experienced handling.

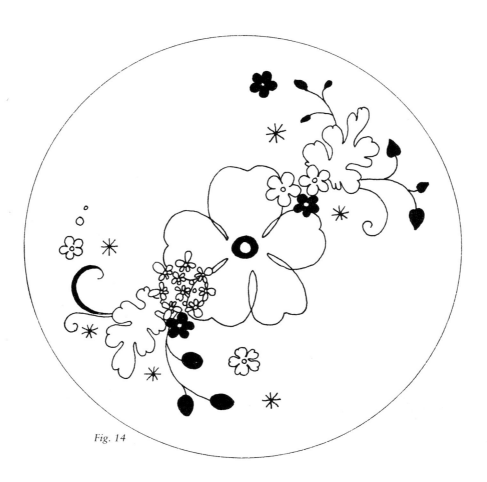

Fig. 14

material. When securing a fully opened flower head, place the adhesive on the spot where the centre of the flower will rest or, if a centre has been removed, place the adhesive near the opening. Never spread adhesive underneath petals because they will pucker when the adhesive dries or when the covering is pressed firmly into place. If you wish, a tiny flower or particle can be placed over a central hole to form an imaginary flower head and single petals can also be arranged into an imaginative shape. According to the manner in which it was pressed, an open flower may appear to be looking in one direction and it should then be positioned so that it looks into the centre of the arrangement or in the main direction, not facing towards the edge of the frame or away at an angle.

Single spray   (Fig. 14)

A single well-defined flower head can form the centre piece of a simple arrangement and, because this basic composition will draw attention to the finest detail, it is worth selecting a perfectly preserved specimen for such a prominent position. The tiny sprays which flank a central flower head often look more graceful if they are arranged in a curving diagonal direction instead of a straight-across line and the gaps between flower and sprays can be filled with smaller flower heads. The tiny clusters of florets such as Cow Parsley, Alyssum and Gold Dust make very useful filling material because they link an arrangement together without disturbing the colour balance with too much density.

Petal prune

A satin-lined lid shows a Delphinium head in full but unnatural glory! The lower petals have been gently plucked from the back until only the appealing, central shapes remain on view. Larkspur is another flower which benefits from this treatment although careful judgement is required to know when to stop. Some multi-layered flowers respond surprisingly well while others fall completely apart in a shower of resentment!

The spray tips are completed with pink flutes of Red Deadnettle with blue trumpets of Ground Ivy in the centre. In spite of the different names, both these flowers belong to the same LABIATAE family. Botany is a specialised subject and because certain flowers have several rural nicknames, only widely used names have been used to identify various plants in this book.

Fig. 15

Circular spray   *(Fig. 15)*

This arrangement is similar to the Single Spray
except that the leaves and flowers are extended all
around the central flower. You will find that
irregular lengths and contrasting curves will
create a lively sense of movement which is often
lacking in designs that consist of matching pieces
spaced apart at equal distances in motif style.

Fig. 16

The floral spray   (Fig. 16)

This curving sweep of flowers and leaves is an arrangement you will probably repeat many times because it is suitable for displaying a wide selection of material to the best advantage. Although it looks complicated, it is only an extended leaf cluster combined with separate clusters as seen in Figure 16.

When you first attempt to make these sprays, it is easy to place the material too close to the edge of the frame. It will help if you place the main flower heads slightly off centre, without fixing them, to serve as a focal guide. The spray can always be widened by tendrils and pods pointing towards the edge and if they are to be fully appreciated, these fine details deserve a clean background on which to stand out clearly.

Fig. 17

Flower garland   (Fig. 17)

In this arrangement, a central flower is surrounded by a garland of small pieces and fragments and it is a useful design for using up
imperfect specimens which can be disguised
beneath the adjoining material. Rich colours, like
those form the purple Pansy or Sweet William,
should be evenly distributed and it is advisable to
fix these first into place. If too many dark or strong
shades are grouped together, they will disturb the
visual balance of the garland. While pencil guide
lines cannot be used in most cases, because there is
the difficulty of removing them afterwards, the
garland is an exception because a thin line will be
covered by the width of the material.

To display this arrangement to the best advantage, leave a clear space between the central flower
and the garland and a clear border between the
garland and frame.

False impressions

The large composite flower in the centre is made from faded petals collected from several Sweet Pea flowers. The larger petals are placed apart to form the main outline, with smaller petals overlapping towards the centre.

This flower is surrounded with a simple border of tiny faded flower heads and clusters which do not distract. An ornate border of bright colours would overwhelm its basic simplicity.

Fig. 18

The bunch of flowers (*Fig. 18*)

Flowers and leaves can be arranged into bouquets
or posies and the tips of the outer pieces should be
secured first, so that the adhesive fixing the bases
of stems and stalks can be covered by the central
group of flowers. Petals of a suitable shape can
suggest the bow and ribbons or the shapes can be
cut from larger petals such as Tulip or Montbretia. The individual flowers from a Clover or
Red Deadnettle make elegant curving stems and
are more attractive than green stalk clippings
which can look stiff and awkward when grouped
together.

Top left. *Small tips of fern do not distract from these well preserved Buttercups.*

Top centre. *Three tiny clover leaves tumble towards Scarlet Pimpernels while a small star leaf hovers above.*

Top right. *Curling Delphinium petals add width and colour into a thin spray of fragments.*

Below left. *The lower half of a circular spray is completed with three strands of Red Valerian, held together with a Forget-me-not.*

Below centre. *A bright red Rose petal bowl bulges with flowers.*

Below right. *A butterfly descends on pink Orchid while a blue Borage flower fades from view.*

Fig. 19

The flower vase (*Fig. 19*)

This arrangement is constructed in the same way as the flower bunch, with a vase or bowl replacing the bow and stems at the base. The vase can be trimmed from a large petal and it is advisable to select a deep colour to make the shape stand out clearly. A Rose petal makes a suitable base and this should be placed into position first, followed by the outer leaves, so that the central flowers can overlap the stems and cut edge at the top of the vase. To create a natural impression, tiny pieces can be secured on top of the petal vase to suggest flowers facing downwards, while minute fragments beside the base of the vase will represent fallen petals.

Living flowers

A lively collection of plant life overspills from a Tulip vase. Two slender heads of dried moss spring between the dark green leaves of the Ivy-leaved Toadflax while a cluster of pink Alyssum bursts free from the bunch. A further sense of movement is suggested by placing a few fragments in the downward, falling position with tiny pieces arranged around the base to resemble recently fallen petals. Stiff stalks are kept to a minimum because too many straight lines can result in a lifeless or stilted composition.

Above. *A small porcelain frame holds an arrangement on blue satin. Because the inside of the frame is slightly irregular and cannot be fitted tightly with glass, the work is protected with self-adhesive film. The base is padded to hold the work in place and the back is sealed with thick card glued to the edge of the frame.*

Uplifting colours

A two-toned dwarf Pansy flower lies between two trumpets of Montbretia. Each trumpet has been carefully trimmed towards the base to eliminate bulk and produce a more graceful shape while the petals remain untouched. The spray is extended with sprigs of Common Sorrel, Heuchera flowers, a faded Hawthorn leaf and Gold Dust fragments. The leaf and florets lift up the light yellow centre of the Pansy which would otherwise be overshadowed by the rich rusts and oranges. Whenever you work with strongly contrasting colours, it is important to pick out the paler shades to maintain the balance of the arrangement.

Greenery has been deliberately excluded from this oval composition because medium and pale green backgrounds rarely accept natural shades with good grace. The colours are inclined to sink into the background or look strangely drained and drab. In contrast, they obligingly display the range of rust and cream leaves to full advantage!

Fig. 20

The garden (Fig. 20)

Stemmed flowers which have been pressed in the sideway position and curve in a gracious line can be shown to good advantage when used in a miniature garden scene. Tips from spiked plants, such as Melilot and Common Sorrel, also provide suitable material and the tall stemmed sprays should be fixed first so that the adhesive at the base can be covered by the leaves and flowers in the centre of the garden. A natural impression is obtained by assembling sprays of uneven height. Exact matching and regularity in flower arranging often results in a stilted, lifeless composition.

Dark Primula flowers and leaves are positioned
on a blue background for the first stage of a
garden scene. After the main colour scheme and
basic outline has been satisfactorily established,
the pieces are secured into place before the final
finishing touches and details are included in the
arrangement, as shown in Fig. 20.

   A frame should always be considered as an
integral part of the presentation, not added as an
afterthought. This light wooden frame was
selected to extend the colours of the leaves. It is a
good idea, when one is working on an
arrangement, to place the frame around the work
occasionally to see how the arrangement is
progressing.

Fig. 21

The forest (Fig. 21)

Small single leaves often resemble the shapes of fully grown trees and these can be assembled into miniature woodland or forest scenes. By framing the arrangement with curving inward shapes, in the manner of a fisheye lens, it is possible to create an intimate glimpse into this imaginary world. Stiff, straight pieces produce a more formal effect. Small flower heads and strands of moss can be included to suggest the foreground of the scene.

Opposite. *A worm's eye view of the miniature forest reveals how the smallest leaves can echo the shapes of the largest trees! This collection of scenes shows how wooden curtain rings can be used for frames and in this case, natural wood suits the subject. For full details on ring frames, see chapter five, page 85.*

Flower figures   (Fig. 22)

Flowers frequently have a sentimental significance but unfortunately the Roses and Carnations which are often presented on special occasions such as birthdays, weddings and anniversaries are unsuitable for pressing in complete form. However, by taking the petals from these flowers, and pressing them individually, you will have the material for a flower figure in period costume with which to commemorate an important event or to present as a personal gift.

When working on a figure arrangement, you should aim for a general impression rather than exact representation. I allow the shapes of the petals to suggest a suitable form. It may take many minutes of moving the material around with a needle point before an outline emerges and then I only secure the pieces which suggest the main bulk and line. When working over a figure arrangement, it is often difficult to judge the proportions accurately or how well they fill the available area, so when the key pieces are secure, I prop the arrangement upright at a small distance away and then judge the overall effect. Quite often, a bonnet is out of line with the body, an arm is too angular or a skirt sweeps too much to one side. All corrections must be made at this stage because no amount of ornate detail will disguise an ill-proportioned or unbalanced figure. The final touches should be added only when the figure is completed and your assorted pack of fragments will provide a wide choice of trimmings and accessories ranging from flounces of Queen Anne's Lace to Sorrel star beads.

Many flower petals, when dried, resemble fabrics, and while large ones can be trimmed into garment shapes with sharp scissors, smaller ones can be arranged in tiers. Creamy Hydrangea petals can be overlapped into christening robes and bridal gowns, Pansies have a velvet surface suitable for evening dresses, and a blue Delphinium petal contains the light swirl of chiffon and Tulip is reminiscent of shot-silk and taffetta. All of these surfaces can be embossed with paper for special effects.

Fig. 22

A paint sprayed mount displays a brown Primula dress with a feathery blue Delphinium shawl. The bonnet is tied with a flounce of Cow Parsley, Lobelia and pink Nettle flowers.

Page 70. A lady wears a costume of Tulip petals with lace trimmings of Herb Robert in the hem of her skirt, bonnet and bouquet. Each petal has a distinct grain running through it which is used on dress-making principles; down, across or on the bias. The inner tips of the petals are sturdy enough to be cut into details, such as the deep brown flounce in the skirt, while the flimsy outer edges are ideal for flowing fabrics.

Opposite. *See caption on page 69.*

Above. *A Rose petal cape and cap with real feathers is worn with a leaf boa and a strand of Sorrel beads. Eye make-up courtesy of Herb Robert Cosmetics!*

Above. *Pale Hydrangeas are worn with a Sweet William petal collar.*

Opposite. *A blue bridesmaid is surrounded with a paper mount.*

Initials (Fig. 23)

Initials are ideal for personal gifts and, because they can be constructed completely from fragments and imperfect specimens, they can be convenient at Christmas when flower stocks are inclined to be low towards the end of the year. Like the garland, a light pencil guide can be used for the basic outline because it will be completely covered with material.

Royal initials are constructed with leaves, flowers and fragments. Herb Robert leaves are used in the straight strokes of the E. Cut-leaved Cranesbill fragments are used for the curves and straight lines of the R.

Opposite. *A birthday paperweight with a personal initial forms a special gift. Tiny Toadflax leaves and tendrils are useful for rounded letters, along with curved stems from Primrose plants.*

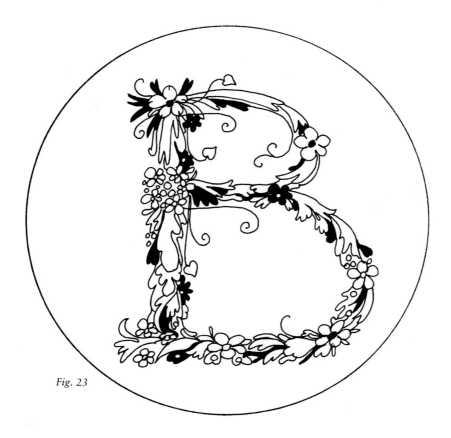

Fig. 23

CHAPTER FIVE
Frames and fittings

Frames and fittings

If pressed flower work is to survive for any length of time it must be preserved in sealed, airtight conditions. While this inevitably excludes some forms of presentation there is still a wide selection available providing the correct measures are taken.

Wooden frames and suitable mounts

Conventional frames can be used but wooden ones such as shown on pages 63, 65 and 71 must be carefully checked for dust. When the frame is wiped clean, sharply tap each side to see if it sheds sawdust or dirt. If the frame is sound but continues to shed particles, bind the raw edges with strips of gummed paper tape. Should the wood prove wormed or warped, discard it.

It is essential that the glass fits exactly into the front of the frame. To prevent your work from becoming damp or damaged in a frame-maker's workshop, it is best to buy the glass from the framer or a glazier before the arrangement has been assembled. Once you have all the frame fittings, the work can be fitted and sealed immediately on completion. A new frame is usually supplied with a backing board but, with an old frame, it may be necessary to have a piece of hardboard cut to fit into the back. Cardboard is not strong enough to use as a backing board but, to create a snug fit, you will probably need to insert sheets of cardboard between the arrangement and the backing board. These should be exactly the same size as the backing board, not slightly smaller because air pockets will form in the corners. Apply card to a level so that when the backing board is placed in position it rests slightly above the back of the frame, not sunken below it – because this will leave a slight gap which will eventually allow moisture inside. All metal clips and screws should be removed from the back of the frame and when the glass, arrangement, cards and backing have been layered, the edges should be sealed with strips of gummed paper.

Because of the sealed factor, a thick card mount should *never* be used with pressed flowers. The petals will soon curl up and the arrangement swiftly deteriorate. Thin paper mounts (see page 73) can be used with arrangements but, because of the difficulty of cutting paper into smooth shapes, it is best to purchase these from a professional source. Glass printed with mount shapes can also be purchased and these provide a satisfactory and very pleasing style of presentation. (See pages 15, 69.)

An alternative method lies in assembling the arrangement on a base smaller than the area to be framed and placing a piece of coloured card, or card covered with fabric behind it so the work is surrounded with a coloured border.

When mounting a picture in this manner, select the coloured card to fit snugly inside the frame. If fabric is being used, fold the edges back firmly and stitch them together with thread across the back of the card. Assemble the arrangement on a piece of professionally cut paper or thin card with the correct dimensions – because it is very difficult to correct the size of an arrangement afterwards with scissors. The edges of the paper will be clearly on display and if these look tatty or out of line, it will spoil the presentation.

Locked frames and fabric backgrounds

Many of the miniatures in this book are assembled in locked frames which are manufactured for pressed-flower work and range from one inch to six inches in size. See pages 25, 33 and 43. The frames can be purchased complete with a perspex covering, a card base, a layer of thin foam padding to place behind the base, a locking plate and a backing card, along with instructions for assembling them correctly. Coloured card can be used in place of the plain card provided, or you may prefer to use an attractive scrap of fabric as an alternative background. From a large scrap bag collected for the purpose, I have experimented with silks, crepe-de-chine, and satins (see pages 31, 27 and 19) and velvets in a wide assortment of colours to show certain flowers to the best advantage. Other fabrics can be used, but it is best to avoid pronounced textures and tones which might distract from the natural shades of the dried material. Always iron the fabric first and if steam has to be used to remove stubborn creases, leave the fabric to air overnight in a warm place. Velvet should also be dry-ironed on the back to make the pile more manageable. See pages 29 and 35.

Remove the perspex, foam, plate and backing card to one side and cut a square of fabric large enough to cover the base card with a generous allowance all round. Fit the frame into place over the fabric and card, adjusting the fabric until it lies smooth and flat in the manner used for fastening

material into a needle work ring. With the frame still in position, assemble the flower arrangement and remove the frame when the work is completed. The arrangement should then be covered by the perspex, but remember, this is a tricky stage as loose petals and particles can easily lift up through static and catch on to the cover. I have found that by wiping the perspex clean with a natural, not synthetic, piece of rag and then rubbing it lightly across my cheek, the material is more inclined to remain in position.

When the perspex is in place, replace the frame and insert the piece of foam behind the base card beneath the folds of the fabric. Trim away the surplus fabric and then press the locking plate into position. If thick velvet has been used, this might be difficult and it will be necessary to remove the frame to trim the fabric away exactly around the

A burgundy based paperweight captures a large, fully opened Thistledown. To keep the work pressed firmly against the glass, padding is placed in between the base supporting the arrangement and the self-adhesive base. Without this precaution, the flowers will disintegrate.

edge of the base card. If possible, hold the perspex in position while trimming and blow away the cut threads while you work because these can easily slip into the flower arrangement and can be very tedious to remove with a needle point. A small piece of self-adhesive tape or film rolled into a circle will be useful for picking up loose specks from a background but do not touch any part of the arrangement because it will also lift this away as well. Once the locking plate is in position, the back card will fit easily into place.

Assembling a velvet mount

Apart from frames, there are other items manufactured with mounts for miniature decoration and these include pendants for jewellery which can be threaded on chains or fixed to brooch fittings, pill boxes, tiny trinket pots, lidded bowls, compact and key fobs. For an impressive presentation, a miniature can be enclosed in a velvet mount. For example, the arrangement on page 82 was assembled on a pot lid and fitted into a frame, both purchased from the same source.

To make a similar mount, you will need the following items:-

One 4-inch lid, complete with locking plate.
One 6-inch frame, minus perspex or glass.
One 6-inch circle of firm card.
7 square inches of quilt padding.
8 square inches of velvet.
A needle, strong scissors, thread: plus the usual

miniature materials with which to arrange the lid.

Use the backing from the frame as a guide for marking the 6-inch circle of card and cut just inside the marked line because the velvet will take up space when folded over the edge of the card. Place the velvet square face downwards and put the card in the centre. Mark one inch all around the card circle, using a chalk pencil if the fabric is dark. Cut out the velvet circle. Thread the needle and double knot the end. Pierce through the velvet so the knot lies on the piled surface ¼-inch away from the edge of the fabric. Make a circle of small even stitches around the edge and finish with the thread running loosely out next to the knot. Make another row of stitches ¼-inch inside the first row in the same manner.

Place the circle of card on the padding, mark the edge and cut out a circle of padding to match the

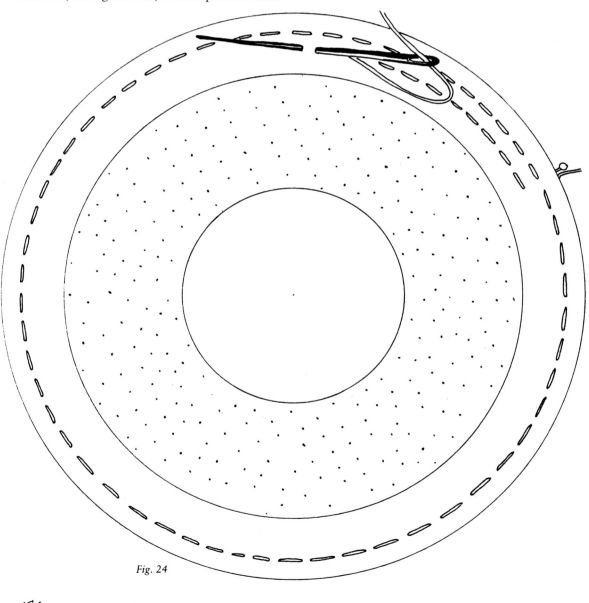

Fig. 24

card. Remove the padding to one side and fit the card inside the frame. Place the lid in the centre and mark the edge, having measured equal distances from edge to edge so the lid is exactly central. Cut out the centre of the card and fit the lid into the opening. If it fits tightly, enlarge the opening slightly because the velvet will take up room when it is folded back through the opening.

Replace the card on the padding and mark the centre opening; trim the padding to match, and then secure the padding and the card together with adhesive. Trim the edge of the padding at a diagonal angle in order to taper the depth. Place the velvet circle facing pile downwards and position the padded card on top with the padding against the back of the velvet. Slowly draw up the threads and evenly gather in the velvet until it folds back smoothly and firmly around the edge of the card. Secure the gathering with small stitches.

Pierce the centre of the velvet circle with scissor points and cut out a circle ½-inch smaller than the centre of the card. Snip into the edge of the circle at regular intervals, cutting just below the edge of the card, to enable the velvet to fold back. Using firmly knotted double thread, catch the two velvet edges together with taut regular oversewing stitches to produce a firm, smooth surface. Secure the thread with stitches, trim away any surplus fabric bulk and fit the padded velvet circle inside the frame. Position the backing card in behind the mount and secure with pins. Apply adhesive in the centre and secure the assembled pot lid inside the mount.

Another presentation can be prepared by simply padding the card as above without removing the centre. The miniature can then be secured to the velvet surface with adhesive, producing a raised centrepiece like that on page 35.

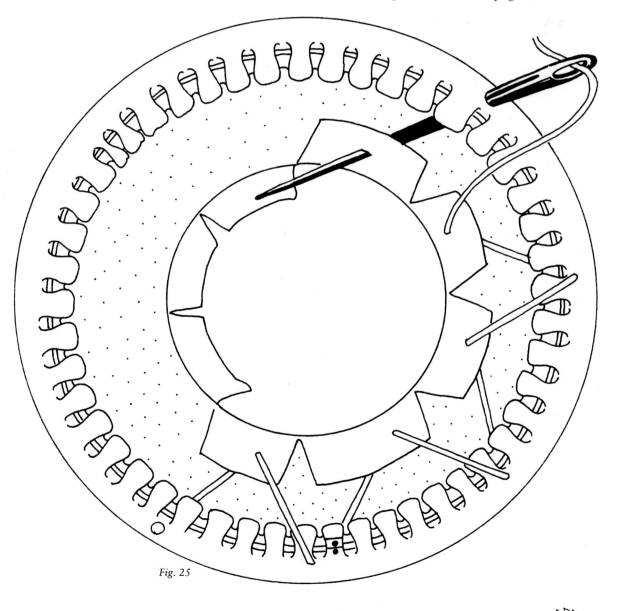

Fig. 25

A different form of mounted miniature displays a
Candytuft flower head flanked with green
Geranium leaves, purple Hydrangea flowers and
Aquilegia leaves with two tiny Trefoils at the top.
Cow Parsley and pink Alyssum clusters break up
the strong, dark colours which could easily
overpower the soft pink colouring in the centre.

   This arrangement is sealed inside a frame and
inserted into a padded velvet mount. Instructions
for making the mount are given in chapter five,
pages 80–1.

Glass paperweights and pots

Miniatures can also be used to decorate the bases of glass paperweights (see above and pages 75 and 79), and trinket bowls which can be purchased in blank form from suppliers. These are supplied with a self-adhesive base which fits under the glass to hold the arrangement in place. The plain base card can be covered with a circle of fabric and this should be cut just fractionally larger than the card but not large enough to cover the entire base because the adhesive on the base will not be able to hold it in place if the sticking area is covered. If a slight gap forms between the pressed arrangement and the bottom of the glass, a piece of foam placed beneath the arrangement base will help to create a snug fit. The colour of the self-adhesive base will be visible around the edge of the glass

A round glass paperweight is lined with fabric which matches the base. When using backgrounds which do not tone in with the base supplied with the weight, it is worth cutting a suitable colour from the range of self-adhesive films.

and if you are using a fabric base, you might wish to replace the self-adhesive base with one of a matching colour. This can be simply cut from a piece of self-adhesive plastic covering available from handyman and decorating centres.

Blank cards with printed borders provide a professional finish for personal greetings. They also remove the tricky task of hand-cutting and outlining.

Left. *A full spray with a centrepiece of two trimmed pink Larkspur flowers is extended with rust coloured leaves. A single pink Heuchera flower balances the lower tip of Herb Robert leaves.*

Right. *A Potentilla flower flanked with trimmed Montbretia trumpets and tips of fern leaves. This very basic spray is lightly completed with two curving Scarlet Pimpernel flowers preserved from a weed patch.*

Curtain-ring pictures   (See page 67)

One of the most attractive forms of presentation I have seen was hanging behind the door of an antique shop, but it was the frame, not the contents, which caught my eye. A few flower heads had been arranged on a small circle of paper and covered with film; around the arrangement an old-fashioned wooden curtain ring had been secured to serve as a frame. Apart from being unusual, it was inexpensive to reproduce and simple to assemble once I had become familiar with working with plastic film.

Old wooden curtain rings can be found in antique shops and second-hand markets and if they are single oddments as opposed to one of a set, they should be fairly cheap to purchase. If the ring is polished or varnished, you will need a piece of medium grade glass paper to roughen the back of the ring. Modern wooden curtain rings can be bought in a variety of natural wood shapes which can be left plain, or varnished or stained with wood dyes which are obtainable in a wide selection of colours from well-stocked handyman shops. Apart from the ring, you will need card for the base, plastic self-adhesive film which can be purchased from stationery departments, a glue suitable for securing plastic and wood and possibly a small gimlet and a screw-eye to repair old rings or replace those which might have been incorrectly inserted into a modern ring. You will also need scissors and a sheet of smooth glass on which to work with the plastic film.

First check the shape of the ring by hanging it against a light background of the screw-eye. Sometimes the shape of the ring is slightly oval instead of completely round and if the screw-eye has been inserted slightly away from the curve centre, it will not hang correctly. If necessary, correct or replace the screw-eye, using the gimlet to form a new opening. On a piece of scrap paper, mark both the outer and inner edge of the ring as accurately as possible and then draw another line in between them to form a guide for the size of the miniature base. The edge of the base must rest against the widest width of the ring if it is to be secured firmly. First make a temporary arrangement on the scrap paper, using the inner edge of the ring as a frame guide and then transfer it on to the card cut to form the miniature base and secure it. Cut a square of plastic film large enough to cover the entire base with a generous surplus all round but do not remove the protective backing until you are ready to cover the arrangement. Dust particles will immediately stick to the adhesive surface and they are almost impossible to remove so place the miniature base on the sheet of clean glass and remove any surrounding loose material. Peel away the backing and place it lightly over the arrangement. Some of the petals will probably rise up through static but providing the film is only resting lightly, these can be very carefully replaced with the centre, not the point of a needle. When the arrangement is in position, smooth down the film with the fingertips, working from the centre to the edges to smooth out any creases. Trim away the surplus film from the edges and spread a thin line of plastic glue around the edge of the base. Place the ring into position, making sure the screw-eye is at the top and in exactly the right place. Press the miniature between two heavy books for a few minutes and then remove it to see if the ring is still in the correct position. Sometimes the glue can cause the ring to slip slightly out of place. Correct if necessary, and replace the miniature between the books to set overnight. For a neat finish, you might wish to back the miniature with a circle of self-adhesive material; attractive flocked plastics can be purchased from decorating shops or felt can make a suitable alternative. Examples of curtain-ring frames are on page 67.

Stationery

Once the technique of covering with plastic film has been successfully handled, it can be used for decorating all sorts of stationery and cards. Writing paper, table settings, menus, invitations, gift tags, book markers and special greeting cards are just a few of the items which can be inexpensively assembled and without a great investment of time.

Many of the decorated paper items on page 87 were assembled on off-cuts of thin card cheaply purchased from a printing shop. Such professionally cut edges eliminate the fuss of ruling out lines and attempting to cut along them with scissors or pinking shears. Neat round holes in gift tags can be swiftly punctured with a leather punch. If required, fold the card first and then add any wording or greeting before applying the decoration. Cut a square or oblong of film large enough to cover the decoration or the complete front of the card, and use the straight edge of the card as a guide when placing the film in position. The ends can be turned over the edges of the card or trimmed level. If you are decorating stationery to be used by somebody else, such as menus, table settings or writing paper, be sure to cover the decoration only and not the entire surface. Inks are very reluctant to remain on the plastic surface.

Blank greeting cards can be purchased from craft shops in plain and coloured card and apart from the floral arrangements, these can be used as a base for flower figures to make delightful wedding and birthday cards. Compared to many modern leisure occupations, flower work is an inexpensive pursuit, especially when composed on a small scale, but each arrangement will con-

Above. *Gift tags made from printer's off-cuts can make an inexpensive and suitable introduction for children's work. The red card in the centre is a simple starting point with two sturdy Feverfew Daisies which will stand up to some sticky-fingered handling. The florist's wedding card requires a more delicate touch.*

Opposite. *Damaged and slightly inferior specimens can be used up on bookmarks, so plenty of bright colours and careful attention to the spray tips must compensate for the small defects. A light sprinkling of Cow Parsley clusters over these arrangements will disguise the blemishes and refresh their jaded appearance.*

tain a degree of patience, artistic skill and imagination which should be appreciated by those who are fortunate enough to receive a token of your workmanship.

Presentation

But if flower work is to survive for any length of time it must be housed in dry accommodation and away from direct sunlight or strong lights. Sadly some people do not realise this until the damage has been started through display in the wrong conditions. Always present your gifts, therefore with brief directions about hanging and a pleasing final touch is to list the plants included in the arrangement. These can be written on a separate sheet of paper or on a self-adhesive circular label which can be secured to the back of the miniature along with the date and your signature.

If your arrangements prove to be particularly attractive, you may be asked to supply a gift shop or store with a large quantity. If you then agree to do this, allow plenty of time in which to complete a consignment because a pleasurable occupation can turn into a nightmare if you are forced to work against the clock in order to meet a delivery dead-line. A happier arrangement might be the occasional stall at a craft fair or a display unit from which to sell your surplus stocks.

Floral stationery awaiting the written word before the protective film is applied. Last-minute afterthoughts cannot be added successfully on top of the plastic coating.

Postscript

Junk and jewellery conversions

If you enjoy searching for natural specimens in unusual places, you will probably find pleasure also in searching through antique and junk stalls for different forms of presentation for your miniature work.

With this purpose in mind, you will discover many items which can be adapted with a little effort and improvisation. The old-fashioned brooches mounted with needlework or coloured prints can be easily taken apart and re-assembled with tiny flower arrangements although you will probably have to replace scratched covers with new perspex.

The oval brooch with the cream background on page 37 (top) was ingrained with grime when I purchased it from a market stall and it could only be properly cleaned by being unclipped into separate pieces. The pendant in the silver scroll mount (see page 37), which is usually fitted with a crown piece, consists of two watch glasses joined together with adhesive. The flowers which appear on both sides are held in place by a wad of foam packed into the centre. The small china frame with the oval centre, on page 62, was intended for a small picture or photograph but it was possible to use it for a satin based arrangement padded

Coloured cards display three well-preserved pieces which are just slightly too large for miniature work: a brilliant rust Cranesbill leaf, a white Iberis flower and a leaf bud originally collected for.its curling stalk.

with foam and covered with self-adhesive film. The arrangement was held in place by a piece of cardboard glued over the back.

In my junk box I have small circles of glass picked up from a glazier after a session of cutting key-holes in finger plates, old lids and compacts fitted with tatty paper pictures, lockets, broken watches, jewellery fittings, cuff-links and buttons along with a jumble of items which have small oval or round inserts. These I hope to adapt into miniature presentations whenever a suitable method presents itself. Such conversions offer an amusing challenge and relaxing alternative to miniature assembly and plant pressing. Like the miniature expedition through an unexplored stretch of territory, the search through rummage will occasionally be rewarded with an object which is perfect for your purpose and like the plants which lie neglected and unnoticed, it will probably have been dismissed as rubbish before coming into your possession.

APPENDIX

1981 list of protected plants

(under the Wildlife and Countryside Act, 1981)

Adder's-tongue Spearwort   *Ranunculus ophioglossifolius*
Alpine Catchfly   *Lychnis alpina*
Alpine Gentian   *Gentiana nivalis*
Alpine Sow-thistle   *Cicerbita alpina*
Alpine Woodsia   *Woodsia alpina*
Bedstraw Broomrape   *Orobanche caryophyllacea*
Blue Heath   *Phyllodoce caerulea*
Brown Galingale   *Cyperus fuscus*
Cheddar Pink   *Dianthus gratianopolitanus*
Childling Pink   *Petrorhagia nanteuilii*
Diapensia   *Diapensia lapponica*
Dickie's Bladder-fern   *Cystopteris dickieana*
Downy Woundwort   *Stachys germanica*
Drooping Saxifrage   *Saxifraga cernua*
Early Spider-orchid   *Ophrys sphegodes*
Fen Orchid   *Liparis loeselii*
Fen Violet   *Viola persicifolia*
Field Cow-wheat   *Melampyrum arvense*
Field Eryngo   *Eryngium campestre*
Field Wormwood   *Artemisia campestris*
Ghost Orchid   *Epipogium aphyllum*
Greater Yellow-rattle   *Rhinanthus serotinus*
Jersey Cudweed   *Gnaphalium luteoalbum*
Killarney Fern   *Trichomanes speciosum*
Lady's-slipper   *Cypripedium calceolus*
Late Spider-orchid   *Ophrys fuciflora*
Least Lettuce   *Lactuca saligna*
Limestone Woundwort   *Stachys alpina*
Lizard Orchid   *Himantoglossum hircinum*
Military Orchid   *Orchis militaris*
Monkey Orchid   *Orchis simia*

Norwegian Sandwort   *Arenaria norvegica*
Oblong Woodsia   *Woodsia ilvensis*
Oxtongue Broomrape   *Orobanche loricata*
Perennial Knawel   *Scleranthus perennis*
Plymouth Pear   *Pyrus cordata*
Purple Spurge   *Euphorbia peplis*
Red Helleborine   *Cephalanthera rubra*
Ribbon-leaved Water-plantain   *Alisma gramineum*
Rock Cinquefoil   *Potentilla rupestris*
Rock Sea-lavender (two rare species)
   Limonium paradoxum/Limonium recurvum
Rough Marsh-mallow   *Althaea hirsuta*
Round-headed Leek   *Allium sphaerocephalon*
Sea Knotgrass   *Polygonum maritimum*
Sickle-leaved Hare's-ear   *Bupleurum falcatum*
Small Alison   *Alyssum alyssoides*
Small Hare's-ear   *Bupleurum baldense*
Snowdon Lily   *Lloydia serotina*
Spiked Speedwell   *Veronica spicata*
Spring Gentian   *Gentiana verna*
Starfruit   *Damasonium alisma*
Starved Wood-sedge   *Carex depauperata*
Teesdale Sandwort   *Minuartia stricta*
Thistle Broomrape   *Orobanche reticulata*
Triangular Club-rush   *Scirpus triquetrus*
Tufted Saxifrage   *Saxifraga cespitosa*
Water Germander   *Teucrium scordium*
Whorled Solomon's-seal   *Polygonatum verticillatum*
Wild Cotoneaster   *Cotoneaster integerrimus*
Wild Gladiolus   *Gladiolus illyricus*
Wood Calamint   *Calamintha sylvatica*

Index

OTHER CRAFT TITLES

GOLD AND SILVER EMBROIDERY
edited by Kit Pyman

Ideas for new applications of an ancient and historic craft. An authoritative text, richly illustrated, which covers the history of metal-thread work, goldwork, applique, machine embroidery, Church embroidery, lettering, bead work, sequins, jewels, stones etc.

MADE TO TREASURE
Embroideries for all Occasions edited by Kit Pyman.

This book offers a rich variety of ideas for embroideries to be made to commemorate special occasions – christenings, weddings, birthdays – from simple greetings cards to a gold-work panel for a golden wedding. A heart warming present precisely because it is specially made.

QUICK & EASY WOODEN TOYS
by Alan Pinder

How simple wooden toys can be made easily, quickly and cheaply, without the aid of an expensive workshop and using only wooden fittings. A practical and enjoyable book which combines clear instructional text, colour pictures, diagrams, and exploded drawings.

THE CHRISTMAS CRAFTS BOOK

Creative ideas and designs for the whole family to make objects with a Christmas flavour: table and room decorations, stars, Christmas tree ornaments, candles and candlesticks, angels, nativity scenes, paper chains and Christmas cards.

EVERY KIND OF PATCHWORK
edited by Kit Pyman

'Really lives up to its title, and is sufficiently easy to follow that even the most helpless needleperson would be tempted to have a go. But there's plenty, too, for the experienced.' *The Guardian.*
Cased and Paperback.

EVERY KIND OF SMOCKING
edited by Kit Pyman

The description of the basic technique is followed by sections on children's clothes, fashion smocking, experimental smocking and creative ideas for finishing touches.

HOW TO MAKE BEAUTIFUL FLOWERS
edited by Valerie Jackson

How to make flowers from all sorts of materials; silk, paper, shells, bread dough, feathers, seeds. The instructions are simple, the materials inexpensive and easy to obtain.

THE SPLENDID SOFT TOY BOOK

The Splendid Soft Toy Book contains a wealth of ideas and pictures for making a wide variety of toys and dolls, from a green corduroy crocodile to detailed traditional, even collectors' dolls. More than 60 full colour pictures and over 70 black and white illustrations show the reader how to fashion appealing figures and animals of all shapes and sizes.
Cased and paperback.

If you are interested in any of the above books or any of the art and craft titles published by Search Press please send for free catalogue to: Search Press Ltd., Dept B, Wellwood, North Farm Road, Tunbridge Wells, Kent. TN2 3DR.